I0169654

Highway Sky

James Brush

Coyote Mercury Press

Austin, TX

Highway Sky

ISBN: 0984920536
ISBN-13: 978-0-9849205-3-2

Published by Coyote Mercury Press
Austin, TX
coyotemercury.com

Highway Sky collection copyright © 2016 James Brush
The individual poems are licensed under the Creative
Commons Attribution-NonCommercial-ShareAlike 4.0
International License. To view a copy of this license, visit
http://creativecommons.org/licenses/by-nc-sa/4.0/

Cover Photo © David M. Schrader/Shutterstock

A good number of these poems originated as snapshots, sketches and memories from road trips taken in the early and mid 1990's, and so I dedicate this to my traveling companions from those days: Thaddeus, Eric, Lara, Séamus, Andrea, and of course and as always, Rachel.

Contents

Part One

Spark

Spark

gasoline fumes

open highways
through memory

endless skies
& stars

asphalt
& awareness

we'll never be
this way again

Early Memory

a bridge rolls
endless over water

cigarette smoke
swirling blue
an open window

Shotgun

shrieking joy and fire
hair snaking out the window
racing parking garage curves
carbon monoxide fumes
tires screech pedestrians
shorebound sailors mostly
jump from her maniac path
cursing the captain's
daughter, her giant car
the course she charted
over asphalt and down
to the drunken shore
down shore drunken
stars sailing overhead
sunrise sunrise bubbling
up from the Atlantic filling
her blonde hair with fire
smoldering laughter spark
the curves of the road, her
body shaking joy and flame
foot on the gas, all the way

Legend of the Wanderer, Part I

He has been everywhere, man. He walks along the shoulder, holding out his thumb. From the Yucatán to the Yukon, the left shoulder to the right, he has seen it all. On Saturdays he goes honky tonkin'. They write songs about him. Call him *Stranger* in Texas and *Buddy* in Tennessee. He hopes to pull the tire jack from the stone and become the king of the road. When Jesus left Chicago, he followed hoping to elude the hellhound on his trail. He still carries the old guitar he found at a crossroads in Mississippi. He tries to play like Robert Johnson but comes off sounding like Elvis. He's met them both out on the highways and told them he was following the Dead. That was a joke, though, and he thinks they knew it. In Luckenbach he joined other wanderers where they sang songs by the outlaw legends until dawn when the sheriff arrived. He hoped to reach Amarillo by noon, but he was running early. He is on the road again, traveling through every road song worth singing. Yes, he has been everywhere, man. Don't you dream of joining him as you lie in bed and listen to cars traveling the night highway?

God Bless Johnny Cash

I drove to the river;
it followed me home.

Sweated the night surrounded
by lesser freshwater demons.

Sang pelagic chanties
heard second hand

from deep-gulleted
birds plucking a thunder bass.

The earth ate the moon,
broke the fall of morning.

Twisted roads passed tallgrass hills
that can't remember trees.

In the morning, I prayed
the dusty pick-up truck petition:

God bless Johnny Cash.

Highway Sky

There was a time when film was too expensive.
In those days, we used words scrawled
on fast food wrappers, creased maps and memory.

The cars ran on gasoline and explosions.
The phones were tethered to wires,
but we weren't tethered to anything.

The highways stretched forever.
Nobody knew what was on the other end.

Not the maps of the ancient conquistadors
nor the atlases of the highway cartographers
could show us the ten thousand things
we needed to see for ourselves.

Because

Because I read Least Heat-Moon, Kerouac and Twain
Because I grew up on Willie, Waylon, Kris and Cash
Because of *Smokey and the Bandit* and *The Cannonball Run*
Because we were learning all the ways you can say love
Because the Jeep could go off road and nobody was looking
Because the high desert wind could have knocked us over
Because the air smelled like pine, and the ground
    was softer than carpet
Because we could be in four states at once
Because you can use a twisted coat hanger to make toast
    over a campfire
Because Zappa's "Montana" cracked us up in New Mexico
Because we knew we'd never be this way again
Because lightning ripped through the space between
    the highway and the stars
Because some roads aren't on the maps
Because the Burger King in Kayenta had a museum
    for the code talkers
Because we saw sunspots through the haze over Houston
Because the Bronco slid into a snowbank during a blinding
    panhandle blizzard
Because the camera fell in the Grand Canyon, and we had
    to have it back
Because we were about to go our separate ways,
    and it broke our hearts to think it
Because the tape got jammed in the deck and so we listened
    to *Strange Fire* and *Doolittle* all the way to Maine
Because the thunderstorms in Denver that summer always
    rolled in at 4:00
Because we knew Garcia wouldn't live forever
Because that guy at Wupatki whispered *Jerry lives*
Because we didn't have cold weather gear for Mesa Verde

Because the perfect bowl of chili was always
	at some diner in the next town
Because in the desert you can see time written in the stone
Because we just left without bothering to make plans
Because that old Navajo man in Monument Valley
	was selling tacos with green chilies
Because we never mistook the miles for friendship
Because a straight line inscribed on a sphere is a circle,
	no matter how fast you drive
Because a train rumbling through the desert can make you
	forget everything
Because when we got there, we missed the road
	and headed back out
Because it can take days to learn the stories inside the car
Because of wind and endless stars
Because she had cancer
Because the sun falls into the sea
Because you laughed when I kissed you
Because we were young
And free

Part Two

U.S. Highways

U.S. Highways

We read lines and studied rest stop signs to
learn the languages that govern highways.

Electric rivers flowed outward from cities
in red trails along the eastern highways.

We lived on the salty French fry grease and
fast food feasts of American highways.

We waited through summer road construction,
rebuilding and slowing northern highways.

In the mountains, we squinted through the dark,
studying switchbacks to discern highways.

Green shadows crept across the road through
endless rolling tree-lined southern highways.

We avoided the rest stop stares of owls
and meth addicts on nocturnal highways.

In the desert night, lightning played with stars,
and we found God along western highways.

The engine downshifted, slow to grip the
road; tires clung like goats to mountain highways.

At night in desert motel rooms we laughed
and followed love down unspoken highways.

Night Driving

In a numberless dreamtime past midnight
on a numbered New Mexican interstate,

tar streaks slithertwist the flowing highway.
Reflected through bug-spattered glass,

daydream nightdream hypnosis distortions
vanish beneath the whispering wheels.

Sleep comes with the insistent wind hissing
poems and country songs through windows.

The moon, falling since Amarillo, descends
to the rhythm of snores. I could wake

the others. Talk and keep the tar from turning
into snakes, but I keep my secrets with the moon.

My foot leaves the gas and the Jeep eases along
the shoulder of Eisenhower's dream connecting

New Orleans bars and Hollywood starlight,
all the emptiness of days and nights between.

The stars across the Milky Way shiver
in crystal air, and I spot satellites, good evidence

of dreams traveling their own highways. I listen
for a coyote's howl to complete my cliché, but

Coltrane's notes, ghosts from the cracked windows,
played when this road was new are just as good.

I smile when Elvin Jones kicks in on "Summertime."
Come morning I'll pass the keys, and we'll sit and rest

awake, together, in the Garden of the Gods.

Over a Cliff

I left a trail of cigarette butts
across Oklahoma. All the way
to Arkansas, I imagined median
fires burning away the past.

In the Ozarks, I backed over a cliff,
spent an hour balanced on the edge
watching my headlights mingle
with the stars while the back wheels
hung over the darkest drop.

Balanced and ready to fall,
I waited for the state troopers
and imagined those cigarettes,
each one a signal fire warning
of all the drops ahead.

Toward Cheyenne

Roiling clouds, grey as the mountains,
spill across sky, over the plains.

Farmhouses wrecked by the violence of wind:
mute warning for those still stuck to earth.

A blizzard's first kiss bends roadside grasses,
travels through tires and axle to my palms

clutching the wheel. I don't remember cars
or birds. Every minute the colors bleed

toward an iron uniformity.
I forget to believe in gravity.

Why Cars Have Brakes

You wanted to ride horses on the beach.
All down the PCH it kept coming up.
You were in no hurry to be back in LA,
but I was in a rush to see it all even though
that meant racing through everything
we saw that long July Pacific afternoon.
And then you got cancer and survived
and changed your life and moved away
but I lost your phone number and email
was something of a novelty back then.
And now twenty years later I'd give
a genie's wish to have ridden those horses
with you that day that sped so fast I can't even
remember what it was like to drive the PCH.

Roadside Attractions

The desert stretches its paws in endless forevers.

Vultures and hawks circle overhead
eyeing faded billboards advertising
diners gone since the seventies.

Echoes of the ancient world tumble
over rock, spill down through time.
Coyotes call those who never come,
hang up when no one answers.

This billion-year-old ocean sea still can drown,
though the water now just floats as clouds.

I walk from my car, leave it unlocked.
I walk over scrub grass desperate for water.
I walk toward rocks painted by ancient hands.
I walk over fish, seaweed, dinosaurs, meteorites.
I walk into time made visible, layered and worn.
I walk until sunset when stars begin to burn my skin.

I get in the car, drive to the next town,
find a motel and watch a ballgame on TV.

A Moment Every Morning

I hold the Styrofoam cup
near my face, inhale
the coffee's warmth.

There's a painted sky,
seven shades of blue
that don't exist at home.

The road is out there waiting,
but I'd rather stay a moment here
in this lonely motel parking lot,
in this forest service campground,
on this broken desert roadside.

If only for a moment,
I'll savor the highway sky.

Clouds brighten in the morning chill,
voices call; the road asks, a ribbon
twisting endless toward the day.

I hold the cup to my lips
and drink.

East in Winter

The sky is the east
bound highway. Winter
trees hold hawks.

How many miles
can we run
without radio?

The engine fades,
the rumble of the road,
its hypnosis.

Weave in and out
between trucks.
There's more freeway

as much ahead
as behind.

Sonnet Found in a Road Atlas

Austin, Waco, West, San Antonio
Carlsbad, Aztec, Shiprock, Tucumcari
Laredo, Lubbock, Winnie, Amarillo
Cortez, Santa Fe, Vail, Mesa Verde
Dime Box, Bellville, Waxahatchie, Reno
Abilene, Dalhart, Nogales, Yuma
Houston, Dallas, Kayenta, El Paso
Mexican Hat, Show Low, Heber, Ozona
Jerome, Sedona, Grants, Truckee, Tahoe
Chinle, Tuba City, Prescott, Parker
San Jose, Monterrey, Palm Springs, Pueblo
Boulder, Tucson, Flagstaff, Port Arthur
Texas, New Mexico, and then Arizona
Colorado, Utah, on to California

Down from the Mountains

sharks   circle   above
        the sunroof
            illuminated   by
lightning

        skyscrapers   like graves
     sprout on the   plains
where   there is   no   water
              only
    cities
       made
          of   dreams

     water   explores the   openings
   sniffing   around
this   conquistadors
  paradise   mud and   rain

     blown in   from   distant
western   deserts fall
     without   mercy
              without
end

     the wipers   slap   it away
as we race   down
     from   the   mountains
before
     it
       turns
         to
           snow

Southwestern Missouri

how clear the water flows
between the sky and stone

imagine a perfect word
explaining math or love
whispered years ago

known only now
as fading echo

ringing off blasted stone
where hills were
sliced for highways

the memory of that clarity
flows along the interstates
over fossil stones

Night at the Interstate Diner

I ran in circles that turned into spirals leading me
back to the same crowds I hoped to escape.
These crowds gathered around holes in the ground,
at truck stops and on famous San Francisco street corners
where they offered drugs and hookups. Did you know
a straight line inscribed on a sphere is a circle?
Driving deep into the night chasing headlights
flickering with bugs, the circles became too much
and I sought crowds in muddy-tile interstate diners
offering tired-eyed cigarette and coffee warmth.
Not conversation, rather a simple acknowledgement
that we're all of us out here, millions, a crowd
dispersed along asphalt lines and stretched so thin
we hardly seem a crowd. But at night, we're
all in the same place. Tired alone worn out
and looking for others to remind us that we're
not the last ones left. Out there, beyond the pooling
rest stop lights, there is nothing. Nobody
you'd want to meet. It's warm here. Stay with us.
Listen to these whispered stories. We'll all be moving on
come morning, a crowd stretched again to the breaking,
forgetful and perhaps just a little embarrassed
that we needed to come together in the long last night.

The Golden Road

It was Fire on the Mountain. We
listened, wrapped in the crackling
hiss of some old tape. I imagined
the strange highway to that sound.

We almost turned around
before Texarkana, the night
so dark. In Little Rock, morning
cereal and the knowledge
that we'd make Knoxville
if we didn't stop.

In Arlington we walked
among the graves. The dead
we didn't come to hear
haunted us to the Dead
we knew were dying.

Fleeting guitar moments, experience
and wisdom gathered into song
blew out on the wind, smoke
in the air, mountaintop flames.
A little bit of music called us east
across a country to hear something
beautiful and true but fading
into darkness.

Surrender

When the headlights
struck the stars

and the radio de-tuned
to static songs,

the highway dropped
away and clouds

grew shapes across
the galaxies below my tires.

And though my hands
still gripped the wheel,

I was now a passenger.

Part Three

Deeper into Texas

A Texas Highway in Springtime

The soaring hawks who patrolled this highway
through the winter watched as wildflowers grew.
As if the sky were napping on the earth,
the fields in spring explode in deepest blue.

Fields mirror sky and fill with the shadows
of hawks and vultures flying through flowers.
Bipedal hairless apes swarm through the fields,
teeth bared, pointing rectangles at each other.

In just a few more weeks, the bluebonnets
will wither and be swallowed by the grass.
Then the soaring hawks will get their fields back
as, ignoring green, the apes just drive on past.

Highway 73 to Port Arthur

salted trees die slow gray
along the hurricane highway

a black waterline stretches
miles across lifeless woods

I-10 Eastbound

chasing a centerline
yellow and fast
it splits through our dreams
but holds us together
static
feedback of a punk rock soundtrack
noise and tears

in that midnight gas station
we were invisible without cowboy hats

eighty? ninety?
outrunning even thought
darkness settles all around
artificial green cheese moonlit skies
above the glittering refineries
seventy miles past Houston
middle of nowhere
cold air
heavy winds
guitar feedback on the radio
then a dying country station
and the whispers of a song

(that first time I wore tie dye)
this road never ends
(now I wear a suit and tie)
it always leads to that same funeral home
(always tears in all these eyes)
in the bayous of east Texas

I listen to your stories
I try to catch your tears

I can't

keep driving
exhale
centerline divides the highway
that makes us one

Road Stones

the road to Houston
firewheels and sunflowers sway
along the shoulder

-

post oak savannah
a flock of scissor-tails flies
south down the Brazos

-

wildflowers grow
thick where the roadside burned
last summer's flames

just east of Houston
laughing gulls replace vultures
this raucous sky

-

grackles rise and fall
leaves in the wild slipstream
passing trucks

.

Deeper into Texas

On a high plains concrete ribbon
(there is nothing) north of Amarillo,
telephone poles stand like crucifixes
after the condemned have blown away.

It's like a whole other country

On the plains of San Jacinto, a story unfolds
in blood, in oil, where Houston routed Santa Ana.
Hundred years go by, blood dries,
and oil gushes forth from Spindletop.

Recoiling back to sacred ground

An obelisk marks the battle field,
but the great refineries offering smoke, fire,
filth to heaven hide it from I-10. These are
the real monuments here: the refineries,

The highways

Rolling on to San Antone—overpriced margaritas,
overdone river walk and Hard Rock Café—once
Mexico's northern town, we visit the birthplace
of our finest ghosts. Remember that old Alamo?

Legends larger than life

Shrine to Texas heroes and the arrest
of Ozzy Osbourne, the church still stands—
tomb of Crockett, Travis, Bowie—besieged
now by hotels, offices, power lines.

Sparking into lucid dreams

They say there's another Alamo near Del Rio,
made for a John Wayne movie set. More real than
the real one, the screams of ghosts and musket fire
still echo, reverberating loudest at the fake Alamo.

Drowned out by open windows

Stopping in at Luckenbach, we down a round of beers.
No one really lives here, but folks come out on Sundays
singing songs by Willie, Waylon and the boys.
Throw back a couple beers with passing strangers.

Let the journey be the story

Under these stars, above old dinosaur bones and
Indian camps, traveling interstate lifelines like
blood through arteries, we find freedom on the
highways, concrete and legend forever

Bind this place to myth

Roadside Artifact #1

Along a southeast Texas highway, alone in a field, a missile points into a blue sky from behind a screen of trees, their lower trunks blackened in a perfect line by Hurricane Ike's saltwater surge. The missile's joints are rusted and whatever markings may once have identified it and warned away godless commies and damned Yankees are long faded leaving behind a tattered egret-white coat of peeling paint. No identifying information lurks at the base unless it's been swallowed by the grasses of the coastal plain that in a less droughty spring would now be alive with the ten thousand shades of a wildflower revolution.

a rusted missile
aimed toward the springtime sky
windblown prairie grass

Since *Lonesome Dove*

Between prairie fire, buffalo and wind
few trees could live here, but some
survived, tall oaken islands over grass.
And when I drive up 183 toward Abilene
some old oak might catch my eye, a tree
hundreds of years old. Settlers might have
known such a tree, Comanches too.
And ever since reading *Lonesome Dove*,
I can't help but wonder at the hard miles
crossed in eyeblink time and what horse
rustlers may once have hanged
from those branches, legs twitching
in the terrible and lonely space above
the springtime blooming wildflowers.

North Through Fog

wheels rumble
the empty space between
night and dawn

a grey ocean over the plains
ghostly signs manifest mysterious
and vanish

punk rock radio
sonic wind pushing outward
a star core against the smothering
gravity of staying

fog covers escape
routes and all directions
are equal

roads disappear into mist
farm and field, town and school,
fast food off ramp, neon lights—
Wichita Falls

Part Four

All Roads Lead Here

Miles (Never Once Imagined)

And we drove for miles.
And we watched those miles
drift away beyond the clouds.

We saw the miles quicken in the purpling sky
above the mountains, rising like beasts
from the steam coming off the engine
outside Albuquerque, again near Palm Springs.

Roofless, without doors, we raced away
from Vegas with just eighteen dollars,
leftover pizza and half a cup of quarters
jingling in the empty back seat.

So we only stayed five hours in L.A.
In the desert that night, surrounded by the
hiss of a cooling engine, we both finally saw
the miles to the stars.

Humbled and freezing in the imagined terror
of that Mojave midnight, I never considered
the miles still to come nor the people with whom
I would travel them.

Just then,
just there,
everything was right.

We had mountains to climb
and never once imagined
we would change our minds.

We Talk of Trains

Road signs riddled with bullet holes,
executed for the mathematical precision
with which they spell out isolation,
define and witness the desert loneliness.

We talk of oceans, beaches beyond horizons,
valleys hidden in the mountains, extinct volcanoes,
ruins and the railroad tracks following the highway.

A crumpled taco wrapper flutters up from the backseat.
Someone grabs it before it escapes out the window.
Dust devils swirl outside, wrestling earth and sky,
spinning proof that everything only wants to escape.

We talk our dreams in circles, always
winding up at the same rest stop, a teepee-shaped
gas station, the movie we'll make when we get home.

A train rumbles alongside us; sharp-edged
graffiti decorates boxcars. We wonder about people
who painted their anger on a train in Saint Louis
only to watch it disappear into the desert.

Albuquerque

Walking low streets, I breathe mountains, morning
air steals into my lungs like piñon smoke.
Soon desert warmth will rule the day. Fiery
storm clouds burn balloons navigating highways
in the sky. I walk conquistador paths,
missionary streets wind past adobe
homes, pueblo bungalows. I imagine
living here. This walk starts an audition,
a yearlong romance with this desert town
made perfect by the fact it isn't home.
Between the Sandias and the desert,
the river and the roads, a place to stop.
Breakfast in a warm welcoming diner:
bagel and cream cheese with fresh green chilies.

Roadside Artifact #2

Near Meteor Crater, a collision of rusted old cars lies strewn across the high desert plateau. It's very picturesque, those ruined cars with the San Francisco Peaks in the blue haze background. You imagine these cars were ejecta kicked up by that meteor that impacted this same land all those millennia ago. So then these cars are not from our time but perhaps belonged to those ancient humans who surely lived and drove and disappeared long before the Anasazi. These cars speak to us like the statue of Ozymandias: *Look on my wrecks, ye restless, and drive.* We recognize our future in the past. These will be our cars someday when our stories will be as unknowable as the weeds sprouting in the protective shelter of these rusted dreams.

desert weeds
scratch against rust
lost freeways

Canyon de Chelly

Indian drums pounding
heartbeats for paying tourists
ripple the fabric of our tent

night falls slow drums fade—
dreams of bears and annotated
histories of faded dangers

come sunrise woodsmoke and coffee
the whooshing collapse of tents
engines mumbling readiness

we drive the rim and hike
down to the White House Ruins
you trail your fingers along the stone

I look through my camera
search for what Ansel Adams found
in those Anasazi lines

I struggle to compose his vision
in my viewfinder while Navajo men
sell dream catchers chuckling as they watch

In Navajo Country

Cars were rare along the highway
On that day of dusty miles.
You came up a ridge behind us to
Observe our speedy passing.
Through the rearview, we watched you
Emerge, then fade back into the desert.

The Wonder

Against northern Arizona's canyon sky,
we stare down at the world below.
Toothpick trees cling to canyon sides;
a hawk screeches out its call.
Sunlight catches the Colorado—
a momentary thread of fire as the
lights of Bright Angel ignite,
a beckoning starlight on the farther shore.
If I hold my breath and hold your hand
and the clouded sky grows gears to slow
the hours into eons, we could pause
erosion and hold the moment grinning
through all the changes and the years,
the road to Flagstaff, Vegas, L.A., home.

Bright Vegas

The day the desert was destroyed, water
sucked from distant rivers sprayed through the sky,
and cars bore pilgrims, moths to the flame,
sedated by slot-machine lullabies.

The stars all tumbled to earth, outshone by
neon casinos and fountains of light
while roulette chances to change everything
spun against the darkest of desert nights.

Now, unheeded prayers to dollars drift down
from the mouths of those ghostlike survivors,
mumbling dreams into urns full of quarters
as taillights depart in night's brightest hours.

Boys with flyers for prostitutes jostle
the stars, shouted down from celestial heights.
Barely burning, they stagger slow down the Strip
cursing this blaze, this apocalypse of light.

All Roads Lead Here (L.A. Stones)

a hundred miles out
the glow of Los Angeles
desert starlight

-

waves and foam
erasing her name
from the sand

-

the sun falls to sea
here at the end of the road
nothing left to say

At Night

Three stars pierce the fog
above this lonely place.
Waves crash on the tired shore.
When the sun rises, if ever it does,
where will we be then?
…in California?
…in love?
Or standing barefoot in the salt foam,
stilled
by the wonder of it all.

All the Way

Asphalt miles vanish beneath ever-thinning treads.
Sometimes a truck passes and the car trembles.
The truck fades, a memory in the rearview mirror,
and in that distance behind us, we see freedom.
In the miles between radio stations, voices crackle
from Mexico from Flagstaff, islands in a static soundtrack.
The lines on the map folded on the dash become
highways through the desert, the smile on your lips.
From pine-shrouded campgrounds to painted ruins,
roadside motels to cars wrecked and rusting in the desert,
and in the night-crashing waves of the western shore,
we learn the meaning of these secret messages:
rhythm of wheels, music of static, your hand on my knee,
the elegant whisper of trucks traveling the other way.

Part Five

Closer to Home

Closer to Home

I drag my tired sweating body high up Enchanted Rock, stare out through the wind at what surely thrilled the Comanche in their day. From this rock in the near sky, I can see the ancient highway stretching gray to the horizons. I remember oceans on each end, all the stories written in the asphalt and the sky between. Civilization seems so long gone only the old man in the ranger's hat remembers anything but vultures, yet home lies just over that hill, down that endless road.

Road Stones Around Austin

highway overpass
the city becomes geometry
resisting the fog

-

black birds huddle
against the leeward sides
of highway signs

-

the sky throws hailstones
pinging and cracking my car
lightning rips the clouds

a red-tailed hawk sits
on the traffic camera
eyes on the highway

\-

windshield wipers
slap the gray curtain
taillights fade

\-

rain snicks the windshield
a monolog of keyboard clicks
books I'm not writing

Legend of the Wanderer, Part II

The wanderer prays for all the roadkilled animals at least
once a day. He's done this for a long time, and it's his habit
now. He bums smokes when he can. He sees (and sometimes
sets with a careless flick of the butt) summer wildfires that
scorch the shoulder or the median. Coming around again in
springtime, he sees the wildflowers growing best where the
roadside had burned. This makes him feel important. In the
summertime he rests among the roadside prairie grasses and
huddles under bridges in winter. Someday he will get where
he's going. He hopes he'll know it when he gets there. But he
has been on the highway for years. You've seen him on your
errands around town and kept on driving. He doesn't mind.
Loneliness and solitude are his beans and beer. He knows
this is how songs are made, where they come from. Maybe
he wants to find a home and forsake the road, or maybe
these are his wandering years, and he is in no hurry. I see
him and offer some food and water and wish him well.

Three Prayers for the Dead

baby bird
struggles for the sky
wheels crunch bone

-

windshield rain
roadside deer skeleton
in lush grass

-

black vulture
a squirrel's wet fur
rain-slick road

Chasing Westward

The vultures are heading west, their slow flying
shadow grace just an illusion of the blank sky.

Clock them. They're racing away fast as thought.
Faster than often-repeated certainties and fears.

They escape with gizzards full, hurtling toward the sun,
shuttling some soul's nourishing remains westward.

Out there, I hope, they'll catch the day that never ends,
the place, I believe, night will never fall.

After sunset, I hear the rumbling highway, cars
chasing westward, chasing dreams, the fading light.

Angels

if there are angels
they must be egrets

brilliant
through the morning
highway sky

Most Beautiful Thing

highway, the highway, oh beautiful thing
flowing under a circling sky
our son asleep, eastbound
wildflower spring, old prairie towns

flowing under a circling sky
blackland prairie, gnarled oaks
wildflower spring, old prairie towns
cedar along barbed wire fence rows

blackland prairie, gnarled oaks
long rolling hills, windblown grass
cedar along barbed wire fence rows
speeding trucks, dusty roads

long rolling hills, windblown grass
our son asleep, eastbound
speeding trucks, dusty roads
highway, the highway, oh beautiful road

For Gasoline

Her name was Gasoline;
she was my goddess.

I chased her down highways
and through years.

Driven mad by her
perfume and shimmer,

her invitation to ride,
whispers of adventure.

She ran me a twisted road
to strange cities until

somewhere in the traffic,
the heat of endless delay,

I stopped
and forgot the road.

But she's still out there and
though her name is cursed,

she still smells like freedom
and wild younger days.

Acknowledgements

Thank you to the editors of the following journals, anthologies and sites for publishing some of these poems:

Bolts of Silk: "A Texas Highway in Springtime"

ouroboros review: "We Talk of Trains"

Carcinogenic Poetry: "I-10 Eastbound" & "Miles (Never Once Imagined)"

a handful of stones: "Highway 73 to Port Arthur"

America Remembered (Virgogray* Press anthology): "Deeper into Texas"

qarrtsiluni: "Night at the Interstate Diner"

Houston Literary Review: "North through Fog"

feathers: "Angels"

A Blackbird Sings: A Book of Short Poems (Woodsmoke Press anthology): "windshield rain"

Synchronized Chaos: "All the Way"

The Lake: "Since *Lonesome Dove*," "Albuquerque," and "The Wonder" published together as "Three Scenes from the Road"

The Poetry Storehouse: "For Gasoline" and "Angels" (where both poems are available for creative remix)

tinywords: "a hundred miles out"

Verbatim Found Poetry: "Sonnet Found in a Road Atlas"

"Chasing Westward" first appeared in my short collection *Birds Nobody Loves: A Book of Vultures & Grackles* (Coyote Mercury Press, 2012), and some of the road stones first appeared in one or the other of my *gnarled oak* chapbooks.

Many of these poems also appeared in earlier form on one or the other of my blogs *Coyote Mercury* or *a gnarled oak*. My sincerest gratitude to all the wonderful folks who read and left comments on these poems.

Thank you to the creators, prompt writers, and participants of the online poetry communities *The Sound of What?*, *Read Write Poem*, and *Big Tent Poetry*, whose prompts inspired several of these poems and where some of them found their first readers.

Thank you to Mark Stratton and Marie Craven for their kind and helpful feedback on the manuscript.

Thank you to my family, especially my parents, Jim and Judy, who drove us all over the U.S. while we were growing up, and to Katie and Jon, my childhood co-conspirators of the backseat world.

Thank you also, and especially, to my wonderful, supportive wife Rachel. In many ways, we fell in love on the road, and our life together continues to be the greatest adventure of all.

About the Author

James Brush lives in Austin, TX where he teaches high school English. He can be found online at *Coyote Mercury* (coyotemercury.com) and Twitter @jdbrush. He also edits the online literary journal *Gnarled Oak*.

Also by James Brush:

A Place Without a Postcard
Birds Nobody Loves
The Corner of Ghost & Hope

www.ingramcontent.com/pod-product-compliance
Lightning Source LLC
Chambersburg PA
CBHW031632040426

42452CB00007B/783